OSCEOLA
SEMINOLE WAR CHIEF

BY WYATT BLASSINGAME

ILLUSTRATED BY AL FIORENTINO

GARRARD PUBLISHING COMPANY
CHAMPAIGN, ILLINOIS

ALICE MARRIOTT and CAROL K. RACHLIN of Southwest Research Associates are consultants for Garrard Indian Books.

MISS MARRIOTT has lived among the Kiowa and Cheyenne Indians in Oklahoma and spent many years with the Pueblos of New Mexico and the Hopis of Arizona. First woman to take a degree in anthropology from the University of Oklahoma, she is a Fellow of the American Anthropological Association, now working with its Curriculum Project.

MISS RACHLIN, also a Fellow of AAA and of the American Association for the Advancement of Science, is a graduate in anthropology of Columbia University. She has done archaeological work in New Jersey and Indiana, and ethnological field work with Algonquian tribes of the Midwest.

Contents

The Seminoles

Osceola's people were not known as Seminoles until about the time of the American Revolution. They were runaways from the Creeks and other tribes who lived in Alabama and Georgia. They were members of the Five Civilized Nations. These were the Southeastern Indians—the Chickasaws, Cherokees, Choctaws, and last, the Seminoles.

They built thatch-roofed *chickees* to live in and each chickee had its own garden plot. They grew corn, beans, pumpkins, and squash. They hunted game and fished the lakes and rivers. Wooden hoes, planting sticks, stone axes, and pottery and clothing were all made by Seminoles.

After the Seminole War, some of the Indians refused to go to the Western reservations. They fled deep into the swamps. Today, the campfires of the chickees can be seen glowing in the dark Florida Everglades.

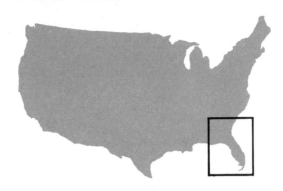

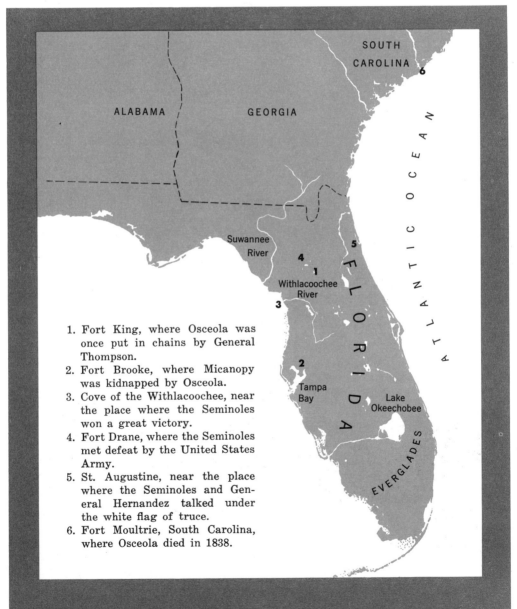

1. Fort King, where Osceola was once put in chains by General Thompson.
2. Fort Brooke, where Micanopy was kidnapped by Osceola.
3. Cove of the Withlacoochee, near the place where the Seminoles won a great victory.
4. Fort Drane, where the Seminoles met defeat by the United States Army.
5. St. Augustine, near the place where the Seminoles and General Hernandez talked under the white flag of truce.
6. Fort Moultrie, South Carolina, where Osceola died in 1838.

1

This Is My Home

The Indian boy let his canoe drift
quietly. His eyes were on the bend of
the river close ahead. A deer stood
there, its front feet at the water's edge.
Its head was lowered to drink.

At first the boy did not move. Then
slowly, carefully, he reached for his bow.

At the same time the deer raised its head. It saw the boy, turned, and disappeared among the bushes.

The boy smiled. It did not matter that the deer had got away. There was plenty of meat in his village.

He let the canoe continue to drift. The river was narrow here. The water was dark, but when he looked straight down into it, it was clear as glass. He could see grass growing on the bottom. The grass moved with the current of the river as if blown by wind.

Now the boy picked up his paddle. He sent the canoe gliding to a willow tree that overhung the water. A fishing line was tied to one of the limbs. When the boy pulled up the line, there was a fish on the end of it.

The boy smiled happily. He took the fish off the hook and put it in the canoe. He put a worm on the hook and dropped it back into the water. "Maybe there will be another fish later," he thought. "This is a good place, a good river. Florida is a good land."

The boy could still remember a time before he had come to Florida. He had lived somewhere to the north, probably in what is now Alabama. That had been a good place too. But white men, called Americans, had wanted the Indian lands. For a long time there had been war. White soldiers had driven the Indians from one place to another. Finally the boy with his mother and a few other Indians had come here—to Florida. They wanted to live in peace.

The Americans did not own Florida. They said it belonged to Spain. The Indian boy did not know where Spain was. He felt that Florida belonged to his own people, the Seminole Indians.

Slowly the canoe drifted downstream. Soon the boy could see the low hill. where the Seminole village stood. Then he heard men shouting. Their voices were angry. One man was waving a gun over his head.

The boy left his canoe at the riverbank and ran toward the village. There were only a few houses, called "chickees." The chickees had wooden floors and roofs made of palm leaves, but no walls. On the ground between the chickees were the open cook fires of the families.

Indian women were busily working near the fires. One of them was the boy's mother. She looked at him with fear in her eyes. "What has happened?" he asked. "An Indian came while you were gone. He brought bad news."

"What is it?"

"White men say this land now belongs to the Americans. Spain has sold it to them."

"The Americans?" Now he remembered being told about the time of wars, when his people had been driven from place to place. "Will their soldiers come?" he asked. "Will they drive us away?"

"I don't know."

The boy turned. Slowly he walked past the chickees to the edge of the low hill. Oak trees grew all around him.

Spanish moss hung in long streamers from their limbs. Beyond the trees he could see the river. On the other side of the river was a swamp. Cypress trees grew in it, their strange, twisted roots rising above the dark water. A great blue heron stood at the edge of the trees.

"This is *my* home," the boy thought. "I will not let anyone drive me away from it. Not ever."

2

Meeting at Fort King

Seminole Indians often changed their names as they grew from boys into men. We do not know the childhood name of the Seminole boy who vowed he would never give up his home. But thirteen years later, when he was a young man, his name was Osceola. On October 22, 1832, Osceola stood quietly under the moss-hung oak trees outside Fort King. He listened while General Wiley Thompson made a speech.

Osceola did not like General Thompson. He knew the general's job was to get the Seminoles to give up their homes and move west of the Mississippi River. Once again white men wanted more of the Indians' land.

Osceola listened carefully while the general spoke. "In the past," General Thompson said, "your chiefs have all promised to leave Florida peacefully. You have always broken your promise. Now the Great Father in Washington grows weary of waiting. You must leave right away."

Osceola looked at Micanopy, the head chief of the Seminoles. Micanopy was an old man. He did not want to leave Florida, but he did not want war. He sat with his head bowed.

"I must have your answer," the general said. "Right now."

The old chief started to speak. As he did, Osceola stepped quickly to his side. He leaned over and whispered, "Tell him you cannot answer now. Tell him you must talk with all the other chiefs first."

Micanopy nodded. "I must meet with all of the other chiefs," he told General Thompson. "Tomorrow we will give you our answer." He stood up. Followed by Osceola and the other Indians, he left the fort.

Fort King belonged to the Americans but it was not much of a fort. There were a few wooden buildings for soldiers inside a high fence. Outside the fence were a few more buildings. One of these

was a small store that sold goods to the Indians and to the few settlers who lived nearby. Another was the home and office of General Thompson.

That night the general left his house and went into the fort. He was angry. "When the Indians met this afternoon, I had a spy among them," he told the soldiers. "The spy tells me that most of the chiefs were willing to leave Florida. But now Osceola is trying to change their minds."

A young officer asked, "Is Osceola a leading chief?"

"He isn't a chief at all," General Thompson said, "not by birth anyway. I don't know who his father was. Some people say he was a white man named Powell. Osceola says his father was an

Indian. If so, he may have been killed while fighting the settlers in Alabama or Georgia. That's where Osceola used to live."

"But Osceola is a Seminole, isn't he?" the officer asked.

"Seminoles are not really a single tribe," General Thompson explained. "Most of the original Florida Indians were killed or died of disease years ago. Other Indians moved here from Alabama and Georgia. Some came to get away from the white men. Some came to get away from other Indians they had been fighting. Seminole means 'one who has broken away' or 'run away.' So all the Indians who have moved to Florida may be called Seminoles. They live in small bands with many different chiefs."

"If Osceola is not a chief, how can he have much influence over the men who are?"

"Osceola is very clever," General Thompson said. "He is a natural leader. But I think the real chiefs will agree to leave Florida, no matter what Osceola may say."

3

Signed with a Knife

As General Thompson had explained, Osceola was not a chief by birth. But he was intelligent and brave. Many of the young Indians wanted him for their leader.

When the chiefs met again with General Thompson, Osceola was with them. The Indians sat in a row on the ground. Jumper and Charley Amathla and many others were there for the meeting. Micanopy sat in the center. Close beside him was Osceola.

General Thompson did not look at Osceola. He looked at the old chief. "What is your answer?" he asked.

Micanopy spoke slowly. "Eleven years ago the Seminoles signed a treaty with the white men at a place you call Moultrie Creek. In this treaty we gave up much of our land. In return the White Father in Washington promised we should keep the land left to us. This is the treaty we wish to live by. We do not want to leave our homes."

"You have signed other treaties since then," General Thompson said. "Two years ago at Payne's Landing you signed a promise to leave Florida. But you have not gone. Now you must go."

The General's words made Osceola angry. He looked at Micanopy, but the old chief sat with his head bowed. The other chiefs also were uncertain how to answer the General.

Osceola leaped to his feet. "That treaty at Payne's Landing was a white man's trick. The white man has broken more promises to the Seminoles than there are raindrops in a storm. We will not leave our homes. Never!"

The general's face turned red, but he controlled his anger. "I speak to the chiefs," he said, "not to an unknown troublemaker." He turned to Micanopy. "What is your answer?"

"Osceola speaks for his people," the old chief said. "We do not wish to leave our homes."

After this meeting more and more Seminoles wanted Osceola for their leader. Micanopy was very old. Charley Amathla was an important chief, but he was timid. Osceola had sworn he would never give up his home. The young warriors knew he would keep his word to them.

Soon General Thompson called the Indians to another meeting. He spread a large sheet of paper on a wooden table. It was a new treaty. The treaty stated that the Seminoles would agree to leave Florida at once. Then General Thompson read them a letter from President Andrew Jackson.

The President said that if the Seminoles did not go peacefully, his soldiers would force them to leave.

"You have heard the White Father's words," General Thompson said. "You must sign the treaty."

Osceola did not move, but slowly, one after another, some of the chiefs went to the table. None of them could write his name. Instead the chiefs made cross marks on the paper. General Thompson was smiling. He looked at Osceola.

"Since you act like a chief, sign the treaty."

Osceola walked to the table. His lips were tight. His dark eyes flashed as he looked at the general. Suddenly he pulled a knife from his belt and stabbed it through the paper. "This is the only way I will sign a treaty with the white man!" he cried.

4

In Chains

About a month later Osceola visited the store at Fort King. The storekeeper was named Rogers. Rogers refused to sell Osceola powder and lead for his gun. "General Thompson has given me orders not to sell any more powder to Indians," he said.

"How does the general expect us to kill game for food?" Osceola asked. "Does he want the Indians to starve?"

Rogers laughed. "Maybe he doesn't care about you."

Angrily, Osceola walked across the clearing to General Thompson's office. There he and the general began to argue. The argument became violent. Finally Osceola turned on his heel and walked out.

The general turned to four soldiers who were standing nearby. "Arrest that Indian!" he ordered.

The soldiers ran after Osceola who was walking across the clearing. His head was high, his face hard with anger. "You are now under arrest," one soldier said.

Osceola did not look at him. He kept walking. Two of the soldiers grabbed him by the arms.

Osceola was not a big man, but he was as quick and strong as a panther. He broke away from the two men who held him. When he did, the other two jumped on him. But holding Osceola was like holding a wildcat. In an instant all five men were rolling on the ground. Other soldiers came running. Finally they carried Osceola, still fighting, into the fort. They chained him to the wall.

For four hours Osceola fought like a wild animal. Then, suddenly, he stopped struggling. He sat there motionless. The chains on his ankles and wrists were bloodstained where they had cut into his flesh. But Osceola felt no pain. He felt only shame and anger, hotter than any he had ever known. It was as if his heart were on fire inside him.

That night, some food was brought to Osceola. He did not even look at it. He looked at the chains that held him— the chains put on him by white men.

Unless he could escape he might, like other Indians, be sent to the west of the Mississippi. But he could not break the chains, so he planned how he could escape another way.

Next morning Osceola sent for Charley Amathla and several other Indians. "Go to the General," he said. "Tell him that if I am set free, I will sign the treaty."

The chiefs did just as Osceola asked. When they had gone, General Thompson went to the fort. "If you sign the treaty here alone," he told Osceola, "none of your people will know. Once you are free, you can tell them you did not sign."

"I do not tell them lies," Osceola said.

"I want your people to see you sign," General Thompson said. "I will set you free if you will give me your word to return in five days. Bring your people with you to see you sign."

"I give my word," Osceola said.

Just as he had promised, Osceola returned five days later. With him were 79 Indians. Like most Seminoles, Osceola had two wives. They came with him, carrying his two small sons. The young warriors who had chosen Osceola as their leader came also. Silently they watched Osceola make an **X** on the paper.

This mark meant nothing to Osceola. He had promised to make it, and he had made it. He had gone freely to General Thompson, and the general had put him in chains. Now he had escaped in the only way he could. But he would not leave his homeland willingly. Ever!

5

Death to Traitors

Osceola now lived in a village not far from Fort King. It was on a low hill with big, moss-hung oak trees. There were a few chickees with cook fires between them. From each fire, logs stuck out like the spokes of a wheel. These logs served as seats. When more wood was needed for the fire, the burning end of a log could be pushed closer to the center.

Here in the summer of 1835 the Seminoles held a secret meeting. Dressed in their long fringed shirts, with egret plumes in their hair, the warriors sat around one of the fires. The light flickered on their dark faces and on the barrels of their guns. One after another the chiefs stood up to speak.

"I do not want to leave my home,"

one chief said. "But if the Seminoles do not leave, the white soldiers will start war. We cannot defeat them in battle. We are too few in number, with too few guns. General Thompson has told us we must bring our cattle to Fort King. We must sell them to the white man. Then we must go to the place called Fort Brooke on Tampa Bay. From

there the white man's ships will carry us west. I do not want to go, but we have no choice."

Another chief agreed with the first, and then another. Now Osceola spoke. "White men have always driven the Indian from one home to another," he said. "If we move west, white men will drive us from there. Finally we will be driven into the sea to drown. If I must die, I will die at home. Florida is my home. I will not leave it."

Osceola's fierce spirit inspired the other Indians. When a vote was taken, they agreed they would refuse to leave Florida. Now they would look on any Seminole as a traitor if he sold his cattle and planned to leave. As a traitor, he would have to be killed.

Not all the Seminoles were at this meeting. Some had already moved close to Fort Brooke to wait for the white man's ships. Others were planning to do so. One of these was the chief, Charley Amathla.

When the chiefs who had met with Osceola heard that Charley Amathla was about to sell his cattle, they held another meeting. Charley Amathla, they said, must be killed as a traitor. It must be done as soon as possible.

Next day Osceola and twelve warriors hid beside the path that led from Charley Amathla's village to Fort King. They had learned that the chief had driven his cattle to Fort King that morning. Soon he would be coming back to his home.

Osceola felt no shame and no sorrow for what he was about to do. Charley Amathla had joined the white men. He was an enemy at war. Osceola was a soldier doing his job.

In the late afternoon Charley Amathla came down the path. When he was close, Osceola gave the signal. The warriors sprang to their feet. No one spoke. Thirteen guns fired all at once. Charley Amathla fell.

"Look," one of the warriors said. From beside the fallen man he picked up a small bag of gold pieces. "This is the money the white men paid him for his cattle."

"Give it to me," Osceola said. He flung the gold on the ground beside Charley Amathla's body. "Let us leave it there," he said, "so everyone will know what the white man's gold has bought."

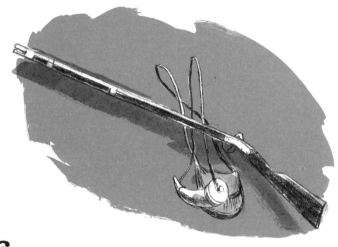

6

Revenge

The Seminole War began. Before it was over, it would be the longest and bloodiest of all the Indian wars in American history.

All across Florida, bands of Indians began to raid the farms of settlers. Sometimes they killed the people and burned their houses. Sometimes they were driven off by the settlers' guns.

Osceola took little part in these raids. "I do not make war on women and children," he said. "I make war only on soldiers."

Osceola knew that to defeat the white soldiers his people would need more guns, lead, and powder. The only way to get these supplies was to take them from the soldiers.

A scout brought Osceola word that three army supply wagons were moving from one fort to another. There were only a few soldiers assigned to guard the wagons.

With 80 braves, Osceola raced through the woods. They hid beside the road over which the wagons would travel. "Wait until I give the war whoop," Osceola said. "Then fire."

Hidden by a palmetto thicket he watched the wagons come closer. A few soldiers rode ahead, a few more behind. Suddenly Osceola's voice rang out, high and thin and terrible. The Indian guns fired. Some of the soldiers fell dead, others ran.

While the Indians were unloading the wagons, some more soldiers arrived. Their

captain ordered a charge. He expected the Indians to run. Instead, they hid in the palmettos and fired back. Outnumbered, the soldiers had to retreat. Osceola and his warriors took everything they could use from the wagons, then they set them afire. In time, still more soldiers arrived, but the Indians had disappeared.

Osceola had never forgotten that he had been put in chains by General Thompson. Carefully, Osceola made plans for his revenge. However, it was not revenge alone he wanted. If he could capture Fort King, he could get guns and food for his people.

On the morning of December 28, 1835, Osceola and his warriors surrounded the fort. They lay hidden in the thick woods, watching. Osceola knew he could not capture the fort except by surprise. He must get inside the high fence.

The commander of the fort did not know the Indians were near. All day he kept his soldiers working on the fence to make it stronger. There was never a time the Indians could cross the clearing without being seen.

46

In the late afternoon General Thompson and a soldier named Lieutenant Smith left the general's office. They started across the clearing toward Rogers' store. The store was close to the woods where Osceola lay hidden.

Quickly Osceola made his plan. He waited until General Thompson and Lieutenant Smith were within easy gun range. Then his terrible war whoop rang out. From all along the edge of the woods, guns fired. General Thompson and Lieutenant Smith fell dead.

Swiftly, Osceola and some of his warriors rushed to Rogers' store. They killed the storekeeper and two clerks. But they did not find the guns and powder Osceola hoped for. These had already been moved inside the fort.

From the store the Indians raced back to the woods. Once more they hid and waited. Osceola knew the soldiers inside the fort had heard the shooting. He hoped that the commander would order them to rush out and learn what had happened. The gate in the high fence might be left open. Then the Seminoles could charge in and capture the fort.

The commander kept the gate closed. When Osceola saw he could not capture the fort, he led his warriors back into the forest. Behind him lay the body of the man who had once ordered him put in chains.

7

Battle of the Withlacoochee

On the same day that Osceola killed General Thompson, other Seminoles were having another battle.

Major Francis Dade was marching from Fort Brooke toward Fort King with about 100 soldiers. They were ambushed by the Seminoles. All but three soldiers were killed. Dade State Park is now located on the site of the battle.

After this battle Chiefs Micanopy, Jumper, and Alligator led their warriors to a place called the Cove of the Withlacoochee. This was a swampy place with many island-dotted lakes and narrow streams. It was about half land, half water. A person could be lost here very easily. Osceola and his followers soon joined the other Indians at the Cove of the Withlacoochee.

At this time the American soldiers in Florida were commanded by General Duncan Clinch. His spies told him where the Indians were gathering. With a force of about 700 men he marched toward the Cove of the Withlacoochee.

An Indian scout saw the soldiers. He raced to tell the chiefs that the soldiers were coming.

The chiefs could not agree what to do. Some wanted to go deeper into the swamps and hide. Some wanted to fight where they were. "Before the soldiers can reach us," Osceola said, "they must cross the Withlacoochee River. We must wait there for them. When some soldiers are on one side of the river, some on the other, we can attack."

Chief Alligator agreed with him. He and Osceola took 250 warriors and hurried to the place where the trail crossed the river. There they hid behind trees and palmetto thickets. Osceola was wearing a blue coat. It had belonged to one of the soldiers who was killed with Major Dade.

Several hours passed. Where were the troops? Could they have slipped past?

Osceola sent scouts to look. Soon one of them came running back. General Clinch's men had lost the trail in the woods. They had reached the river two miles downstream from the ford. At that point the river was too deep to wade. But the soldiers had found an old canoe. They were crossing the river in it, a few men at a time.

Quickly Osceola led the Indians
downstream. Soon they could see the
soldiers. Some were trying to build a
bridge of logs. One man was paddling
the canoe back and forth. He would
pick up six men on the north bank and
take them to the south bank. Then he
would paddle back for more. About 200
soldiers had already crossed.

Osceola told his warriors to slip through the trees and surround the soldiers on the south bank. Before they could do this, someone shouted, "Indians!" Both sides opened fire.

Most of the Indians were hidden along the edge of a swamp. The soldiers were in a small clearing near the riverbank. These were brave, well-trained army regulars. When General Clinch ordered a charge, they rushed at the swamp. Their bayonets gleamed in the sunlight.

Osceola ordered his men to fade back into the swamp, shooting as they went. The soldiers did not want to follow the Seminoles into the swamp. They returned to the clearing. Now Osceola shouted for his men to advance. Once more they fired on the troops caught in the open.

Time and again the soldiers saw the flash of Osceola's blue coat. They heard his wild war cry. A bullet struck Osceola in the hand, but he kept on fighting.

Soon many of the soldiers on the south bank were killed or wounded. General Clinch ordered his men to retreat. They hurried over the crude bridge that had been finished during the fighting. The Seminoles had won the battle.

That night there was much singing and wild dancing in the Cove of the Withlacoochee. Osceola sang and danced with the others, but his mind was busy. He knew that when one soldier was killed, ten others might take his place. One victory did not win a war.

8

Sickness at Fort Drane

As the Seminole War went on, President Jackson sent more and more soldiers into Florida. They built new forts along the trails. From these forts they marched against the small Indian villages.

The Seminoles did not have enough men or guns to defeat the soldiers in open battle. They could only fight briefly, then retreat into the swamps.

They took their women and children with them, leaving the towns empty. The soldiers captured and burned Osceola's town. They burned the towns of Micanopy, Jumper, and other chiefs who would not agree to leave Florida. In turn, the Seminoles burned the homes of settlers. They attacked any small bands of soldiers they found outside of the forts.

At a place called Fort Drane many of the troops became ill with malaria. The commanding officer died. Others were too sick to fight. The able soldiers, carrying the sick with them, moved to another fort.

Osceola did not know why the Americans had left Fort Drane. He did not know that malaria had swept the fort. As soon as the Americans left, Osceola and his followers moved into the fort.

Soon Osceola became sick. First he felt cold, even in the hottest sunshine. His whole body shook as if he were freezing. Then, strangely, he began to feel hot. He burned with a high fever. Sometimes he felt as if he were floating in space. He could not think clearly.

After a few hours the fever passed and Osceola felt well again. But a few days later he had another attack, and then another. He would never be really well again.

One day an Indian scout came racing into Fort Drane. He told Osceola there were soldiers only a few miles away. They were going to attack.

Quickly Osceola called everyone inside the fort. The warriors took their places behind the high fence that surrounded the buildings. Only a few of them had guns. But the fence would protect them, Osceola thought. Firing from behind it, they could hold off the soldiers.

The soldiers, however, did not charge the fort. Instead, they opened fire with one small cannon. The cannonballs

knocked down part of the fence. The balls smashed into the buildings, killing men and women.

Osceola and all his warriors fought bravely, but they could not stand against the cannon. Osceola told the women and children to slip away on the far side of the fort. There was a swamp close by. The women and children disappeared into it. When they were safe, Osceola and his warriors slipped away too.

9

Kidnapped

All that fall and winter the Seminoles lived like hunted animals. They traveled in small bands. Wherever they went, the white soldiers followed. Often the soldiers used bloodhounds to track down the Indians. They drove them from their villages and burned the chickees. They killed many of the warriors and captured many women and children.

Those who were captured were sent west. Those who escaped fled to new hiding places. There was no time to plant gardens. The Indians were always hungry. Many of them had no clothes.

Osceola was sick much of the time now. But between the spells of chills and fever, his head was as clear as ever. He knew now that the Seminoles could never defeat the soldiers. He wanted peace. He had never been in favor of war except to defend his home country. But he would not surrender.

Several times Osceola sent messages to the army generals. Sometimes he met with them himself under a flag of truce. This was a white flag that meant both sides agreed to meet and talk without fighting. Osceola promised that if his people could stay in Florida, they would end the war.

Each time the generals refused. There could be no peace, they said, until all the Seminoles moved west.

By the summer of 1837 most of the Seminole chiefs were ready to surrender. Their people were starving. They had little powder or lead for their guns.

In despair Micanopy, Jumper, and other chiefs led their people to Fort Brooke. Before long, 700 Seminoles were camped near the fort. General Thomas Jesup was now commanding the soldiers. He sent for ships from New Orleans to carry the Indians west.

Osceola had not gone to Fort Brooke. Instead, he and a chief named Arpeika met in a swamp somewhere in central

Florida. Both men were thin from lack of food. Fever had sunk Osceola's eyes deep in his face. "If Micanopy, Jumper, and their bands leave Florida," Osceola said, "we will not have enough men left to fight."

"How can we stop them?" Arpeika asked.

"If Micanopy were to disappear, his people would not wait for the ships. They would go back to the swamps."

Arpeika looked at Osceola. "How do we make the old chief disappear?"

"How many warriors do we have?"

Arpieka thought awhile. "With yours and mine . . . about 200."

"That will be enough," Osceola said. "Micanopy's braves will not want to fight us."

A few nights later Osceola, Arpeika, and their warriors slipped out of the trees near the fort and into Micanopy's camp. They went quietly to the chickee where the old chief slept. They shook him awake. "Come," Osceola said.

Chief Micanopy knew why they were there. "No," he said, "I have given my word to General Jesup."

Osceola made a signal. Four strong warriors grabbed the old chief. They put him on a horse and led him away from camp. Other warriors captured Chief Jumper the same way. The chiefs were not hurt, but they were taken away from Fort Brooke.

The next morning all the Seminoles who were camped near the fort learned what had happened. Without their leaders they did what Osceola had expected them to do. They slipped away from the camp and disappeared into the forest.

10

Captured

General Thomas Jesup was furious when he learned Micanopy and Jumper had been kidnapped. He ordered his soldiers to chase the Seminoles harder than ever. In the next few months many Indians were killed or captured.

Osceola and his band traveled across Florida. They hid in a swamp near St. Augustine. Many were starving. Some, like Osceola, were sick much of the time.

The general in command at St. Augustine was named Joseph Hernandez. Osceola sent him a peace pipe and a white egret plume. Along with these, he sent a message saying he wished to talk under a flag of truce.

General Jesup was in St. Augustine at this time. So he ordered General Hernandez to meet Osceola. If Osceola refused to surrender, General Jesup said, the Indians were to be captured in spite of the flag of truce.

On the day of October 21, 1837, General Hernandez and a few officers rode toward Osceola's camp. They could see the white flag flying from a tall pole. Beneath the flag, stood Osceola. With him were thirteen other chiefs and 71 warriors.

Osceola looked thin and sick. But he stepped forward and shook hands with General Hernandez. "We talk in peace," Osceola said.

"Are you ready to leave Florida?" the general asked.

Once more Osceola tried to explain. The Seminoles wanted peace. They were willing to stay in the swamps and in places white men did not need. But they did not want to leave Florida.

General Hernandez became angry. "You must promise to go at once!" he shouted.

The fever burned in Osceola's eyes. His throat was tight. He tried to speak. Then he turned to Chief Alligator. "I feel choked," he said. "You must speak for me."

As Alligator began to speak, General
Hernandez waved his arm. From out of
the woods, where they had been hiding,
200 soldiers came galloping on horses.
Their guns were ready. They surrounded
the Indians. There was nothing the
Indians could do but surrender.

Osceola looked at General Hernandez.
"Is this the way you treat the flag of
truce?" his eyes seemed to say.

The general looked down. Perhaps he was ashamed of what he had done, but he was following the orders of General Jesup.

Because Osceola was sick, he was put on a horse. Then he and the other Indians were taken to Fort Marion. This was a huge fort built by the Spanish many years before and then known as Fort San Marcus. It is still standing, and you can visit the room where Osceola was held prisoner.

After two months in Fort Marion, Osceola and several other chiefs were sent to Fort Moultrie near Charleston, South Carolina. Here his two wives and his small sons were allowed to join him.

To his surprise, Osceola found that he was famous. Many white people had read about his long fight for his homeland. Many of them were angry and ashamed at the way he had been captured. Well-known newspapers wrote stories about him. Famous artists painted his picture.

None of this meant anything to Osceola. He longed for the dark rivers and moss-hung forests of his home. But he was too sick now to try to escape.

On the night of January 30, 1838, he could no longer speak. By a motion of his hand he told his wives to bring his best clothes. Slowly, with great effort, he got to his feet. He put on his long fringed war shirt, his leggings, and his moccasins. He buckled on his war belt with its shot pouch and powderhorn. He thrust his knife in his belt.

Osceola looked at his wives. Somehow they understood what he wanted. Quickly they brought the other Seminole chiefs. They brought the army officers of the fort. All of them stood quietly in the half-dark room, looking at Osceola.

While they watched, Osceola painted half his face and the backs of his hands with red paint. It was the sign of the warpath, the promise never to turn back. With great dignity he shook hands with the chiefs and the army officers. Gently he touched his wives and his two sons.

Now he could no longer stand. Very slowly he lay back upon his bed. With his right hand he drew the knife from his belt. Holding it, he crossed his hands on his chest. A few moments later he was dead.

After Osceola's death the Seminoles who were left in Florida continued to fight. Little by little most of them were killed or captured. At last the American Army decided there were not enough Indians left to worry about. The Seminole War, the generals said, was over.

Even so, a few Seminoles remained. They made their homes deep in the Everglades. Seminoles are still in Florida today. They no longer make war against the United States. Instead, they live in peace, as Osceola had wanted. But like Osceola, they have never surrendered.